My United States

Wisconsin

VICKY FRANCHINO

Children's Press®
An Imprint of Scholastic Inc.

Content Consultant

James Wolfinger, PhD, Associate Dean and Professor
College of Education, DePaul University, Chicago, Illinois

Library of Congress Cataloging-in-Publication Data
Names: Franchino, Vicky, author.
Title: Wisconsin / by Vicky Franchino.
Description: New York, NY : Children's Press, 2018. | Series: A true book | Includes bibliographical references and index.
Identifiers: LCCN 2017025790 | ISBN 9780531231739 (library binding) | ISBN 9780531247242 (pbk.)
Subjects: LCSH: Wisconsin—Juvenile literature.
Classification: LCC F581.3 .F74 2018 | DDC 977.5—dc23
LC record available at https://lccn.loc.gov/2017025790

1 2 3 4 5 6 7 8 9 10 R 27 26 25 24 23 22 21 20 19 18

Front cover: Dairy farm
Back cover: Hot air balloons

Welcome to Wisconsin

Find the Truth!

Everything you are about to read is true **except** for one of the sentences on this page.

Which one is **TRUE**?

T or F Europeans first came to Wisconsin in the 1800s.

T or F Wisconsin is home to one of the world's biggest annual music festivals.

UNITED STATES

Wisconsin

WISCONSIN
GR8LIFE
• America's Dairyland •

Find the answers in this book.

3

Contents

THE **BIG** TRUTH!

Wood violet

What Represents Wisconsin?

Badger

Milwaukee Art Museum

3 History

4 Culture

Sweet corn

This Is Wisconsin!

N W E S

SUPERIOR

Apostle Islands

①

Manitou Falls

MICHIGAN

St. Croix

Flambeau

Timm's Hill

Northern Highland

CAMERON

Pioneer Village Museum

③

Menominee

WISCONSIN

Green Bay

Door County

EAU CLAIRE

Central Plain

WAUSAU

Chippewa

Wisconsin

Lambeau Field

Oneida Nation Museum

GREEN BAY

Mississippi River

APPLETON

Fox

MANITOWOC

MINNESOTA

Mississippi

Lake Winnebago

Wisconsin Maritime Museum

0   60

Miles

LA CROSSE

Circus World Museum

②

Lizard Mound State Park

LAKE MICHIGAN

BARABOO

Taliesin Home

MADISON

West Bend

MILWAUKEE

Wisconsin State Fair

WEST ALLIS

④

Wisconsin

House on the Rock

Wisconsin State Capitol

RACINE

Racine Reef Lighthouse

IOWA

ILLINOIS

6

① Apostle Islands

This national lakeshore in northern Wisconsin has 21 islands and nine lighthouses. Visitors can camp, hike, kayak, and scuba dive. They can also visit sea caves and learn about shipwrecks.

② Circus World Museum

Baraboo was once the winter home of the Ringling Brothers Circus. Camels and elephants walked the town's streets. Today, circus fans can see memorabilia and attend a big top show.

KE
ON

③ Death's Door

Wild winds and strong currents earned this stretch of Lake Michigan its name. Many ships were damaged or destroyed when sailors tried to navigate the area.

④ Summerfest

Each year close to a million music lovers attend this festival in Milwaukee. Held every year since 1967, it is one of the 10 biggest music festivals in the world.

CANADA

AKE ERIE

Wisconsin is home to some 70,000 farms.

CHAPTER 1

Land and Wildlife

Wisconsin is best known for its rich farmland and green, rolling hills, but there's much more to discover in this beautiful state. Northern Wisconsin is covered with dense forests. The state's highest point, Timm's Hill, is found here. It stands 1,952 feet (595 meters) high. Southwestern Wisconsin is known as the Driftless Area. It's the only part of the state that wasn't smoothed over by glaciers long ago.

Water Everywhere!

Much of Wisconsin is bordered by large bodies of water. In the northwestern corner is Lake Superior, one of the five Great Lakes. Another is Lake Michigan, which makes up Wisconsin's eastern boundary. The Mississippi and St. Croix rivers run along the western edge of the state. The state also contains more than 15,000 lakes and 12,000 rivers and streams.

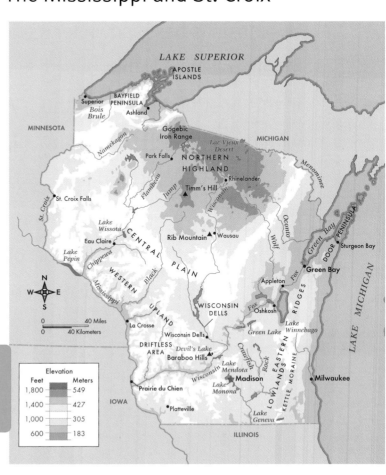

This map shows where the higher (orange) and lower (green) areas are in Wisconsin.

LAKE SUPERIOR
APOSTLE ISLANDS
Superior
BAYFIELD PENINSULA
Bois Brule
Ashland
MINNESOTA
Namékagon
Gogebic Iron Range
Lac Vieux Desert
MICHIGAN
Park Falls
NORTHERN HIGHLAND
Menominee
Rhinelander
Flambeau
Jump
Timm's Hill
St. Croix
St. Croix Falls
Lake Wissota
CENTRAL
Rib Mountain
Wausau
Wisconsin
Oconto
Green Bay
DOOR PENINSULA
Sturgeon Bay
Eau Claire
Chippewa
Lake Pepin
WESTERN
Black
PLAIN
Wolf
Fox
Green Bay
N W E S
Mississippi
UPLAND
Appleton
RIDGES
LAKE MICHIGAN
WISCONSIN DELLS
Fox
Oshkosh
0 40 Miles
0 40 Kilometers
La Crosse
Wisconsin Dells
Green Lake
Lake Winnebago
DRIFTLESS AREA
Devil's Lake
Baraboo Hills
Crawfish
EASTERN
Elevation
Feet Meters
1,800 — 549
1,400 — 427
1,000 — 305
600 — 183
Prairie du Chien
Wisconsin
Lake Mendota
Madison
Lake Monona
Rock
KETTLE MORAINE
LOWLANDS
Milwaukee
IOWA
Platteville
Lake Geneva
ILLINOIS

The Ice Age National Scenic Trail

Large sheets of ice called glaciers once covered much of Wisconsin. As the glaciers melted, they left behind hills, valleys, and **gorges**. Located in southeast Wisconsin, the Ice Age Trail marks the edge of the glaciers' path. It is one of just 11 National Scenic Trails in the United States. The entire trail is about 1,200 miles (1,931 kilometers) long, but only half of it has been marked. Most sections of the trail are out in the country, but some pass right through towns.

ICE AGE TRAIL

POINT BEACH SEGMENT

ICE AGE
NATIONAL SCENIC TRAIL

The Cana Island Lighthouse has been in continuous use since 1869.

There are 11 historic lighthouses in Door County.

Coastlines and Beaches

Wisconsin is shaped like a giant mitten. The mitten's thumb is a region called the Door **Peninsula**. This county has more than 300 miles (483 km) of shoreline and more than 50 beaches. In the summer and fall, the area is crowded with tourists who come to enjoy its natural beauty.

Hot, Cold, and Everything in Between

Wisconsin has four distinct seasons. Winter is very cold, with temperatures often dipping below 0 degrees Fahrenheit (–18 degrees Celsius). Some parts of the state get more than 100 inches (254 centimeters) of snow. Spring brings warmer temperatures and plenty of rain. Summer can be very hot and humid. Fall means cooler temperatures, shorter days, and beautiful autumn leaves.

Some caves along the edges of Lake Superior can only be reached by walking across the frozen lake during winter.

MAXIMUM TEMPERATURE
114°F

MINIMUM TEMPERATURE
-55°F

Forests and Flowers

Trees are found in every part of Wisconsin. Pines and other conifers have cones and needles. They stay green all year long. Maple, hickory, beech, elm, ash, and oak trees are deciduous. This means their leaves change color and fall off each autumn. Many beautiful wildflowers, grasses, and wild plants also cover the land. Spring flowers include wood violets, bluebells, and trillium. In the summer, look for wild phlox, milkweed, and Indian pipe.

The emerald ash borer beetle has destroyed many of Wisconsin's ash trees.

About 28,000 black bears roam Wisconsin's wilderness.

Wisconsin Wildlife

Karner blue butterfly

Wisconsin is full of wild creatures that slither, fly, leap, and swim. Rabbits, squirrels, and a wide variety of insects are found in most backyards. Wild turkeys, foxes, raccoons, and deer are sometimes found there too. More than 20,000 black bears live in Wisconsin's north woods. Hundreds of bird species can be found near water, bogs, forests, and farmland. Birds such as robins and cardinals are common throughout the state. Rarer species include the trumpeter swan and the bald eagle.

Madison has been Wisconsin's capital for most of the state's history. But for a short time in 1836, the capital was Belmont.

16

CHAPTER 2

Government

Does this building look familiar? Modeled after the U.S. Capitol in Washington, D.C., it is the fourth building to sit on Wisconsin's Capitol Square. The capitol has a dome and four wings. The dome is 265 feet (81 m) tall. On top is a 15-foot (4.6-m) statue of a woman wearing a helmet with a badger on top. The statue is named simply *Wisconsin*.

For the People

Wisconsin's government has three branches that work together to protect the people who live in the state. The governor is the head of the executive branch. This branch carries out laws and creates the budget. The legislative branch is made up of the Senate and the Assembly. It creates Wisconsin's laws. The judicial branch, made up of the state's court system, interprets and enforces the law.

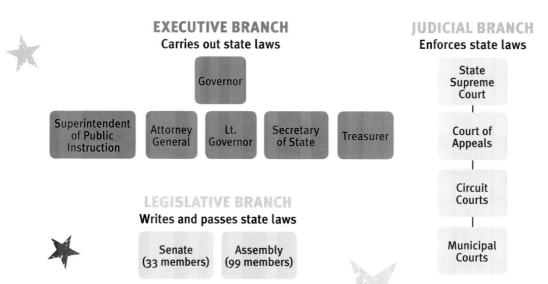

WISCONSIN'S STATE GOVERNMENT

EXECUTIVE BRANCH
Carries out state laws

Governor

Superintendent of Public Instruction | Attorney General | Lt. Governor | Secretary of State | Treasurer

LEGISLATIVE BRANCH
Writes and passes state laws

Senate (33 members) | Assembly (99 members)

JUDICIAL BRANCH
Enforces state laws

State Supreme Court

Court of Appeals

Circuit Courts

Municipal Courts

Thousands of Wisconsin residents gathered at the capital to protest Act 10 in March 2011.

Act 10

In 2011, Wisconsin's governor signed Act 10. This new law meant state employees would pay more money for their health insurance. It also took away collective bargaining. This was a way for **union** members to work together when they wanted to make a change. Supporters felt Wisconsin needed Act 10 because the state was running out of money. Opponents felt that the law took away workers' rights.

Wisconsin's National Role

Each state elects officials to represent it in the U.S. Congress. Like every state, Wisconsin has two senators. The U.S. House of Representatives relies on a state's population to determine its numbers. Wisconsin has eight representatives in the House.

Every four years, states vote on the next U.S. president. Each state is granted a number of electoral votes based on its number of members of Congress. With two senators and eight representatives, Wisconsin has 10 electoral votes.

2 senators and 8 representatives

10 electoral votes

With ten electoral votes, Wisconsin's voice in presidentia elections is average compared to other states.

Representing Wisconsin

Elected officials in Wisconsin represent a population with a range of interests, lifestyles, and backgrounds.

Ethnicity (2016 estimates)

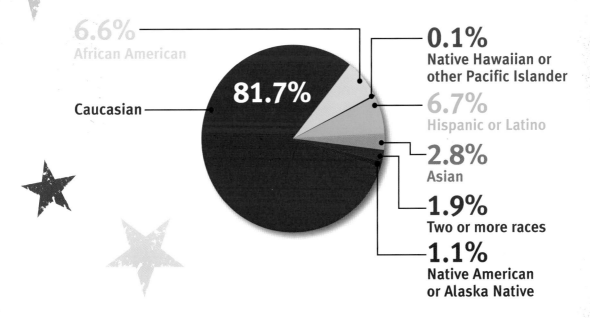

6.6%
African American

Caucasian — **81.7%**

0.1%
Native Hawaiian or other Pacific Islander

6.7%
Hispanic or Latino

2.8%
Asian

1.9%
Two or more races

1.1%
Native American or Alaska Native

68.1% own their own homes.

70% live in cities.

27.8% of the population have a degree beyond high school.

91% of the population graduated from high school.

8.7% speak a language other than English at home.

What Represents Wisconsin?

States choose specific animals, plants, and objects to represent the values and characteristics of the land and its people. Find out why these symbols were chosen to represent Wisconsin or discover surprising curiosities about them.

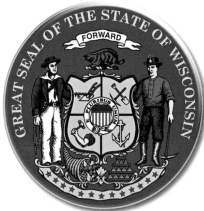

Seal

Most of the images on Wisconsin's seal are related to the industries that are important to the state. These include farming, mining, manufacturing, and shipping. The seal also includes the state motto, "Forward," and the state animal, the badger.

Flag

Wisconsin's state flag has the same design as its state seal. This design was adopted in 1913. In 1979, the state made two changes to the flag. It added "Wisconsin" above the seal and "1848" below the seal.

Wood Violet

STATE FLOWER

The wood violet is a beautiful purple flower that grows across most of Wisconsin.

Honeybee

STATE INSECT

Honeybees feed on sweet nectar produced by Wisconsin's many wildflowers.

Corn

STATE GRAIN

More than 500 million bushels of corn were harvested in Wisconsin in 2015.

Badger

STATE ANIMAL

These mammals use their long claws to dig underground dens throughout the state.

Trilobite

STATE FOSSIL

Trilobites were large, aquatic animals related to today's insects, lobsters, and shrimp.

Kringle

STATE PASTRY

Danish immigrants in Wisconsin introduced kringles, delicious, flaky, and buttery pastries filled with fruit or other sweet flavors.

French explorer Jean Nicolet met Wisconsin's Native Americans when he landed on the shore of Lake Michigan in 1634.

CHAPTER 3

History

In 1897, a Wisconsin family made an amazing discovery when they dug up bones from a mastodon. Mastodons were gigantic, elephant-like creatures that last roamed the earth more than 12,000 years ago. The family also found spear points near the skeleton. This was an even more exciting discovery. It proved that humans who knew how to use tools had lived in Wisconsin a very long time ago.

The First People

Wisconsin was once a very cold place, full of icy glaciers. Earth got warmer over time, and the glaciers melted. About 11,000 years ago, the glaciers disappeared. Soon, more animals and plants were able to survive in what is now Wisconsin. The first people to arrive in the area were **nomads**. They hunted animals for food and followed them from place to place. **Archaeologists** call these early people Paleo-Indians.

This map shows some of the major tribes that lived in what is now Wisconsin before Europeans came.

Ojibwe people lived in homes called wigwams. Wigwams were wooden frames covered in cloth, animals skins, or other materials.

Settling Down

As it became easier to grow crops, Native Americans stopped traveling in search of food. They started to build settlements and trade with other groups. The earliest Wisconsinites included the Menominee, Potawatomi, Ojibwe, and Ho-Chunk peoples. They built canoes out of birch trees. They also used birchbark to cover their houses and make baskets.

European Settlers

Europeans began arriving in the area in the early 1600s. Jean Nicolet, a French explorer, is the first European known to have visited what is now Wisconsin. Nicolet realized quickly that the area was good for hunting. He set up a post to trade for furs. Soon, France and Great Britain were fighting over this rich new land. The British gained control of Wisconsin in 1763.

This map shows routes European explorers took as they explored and settled what is now Wisconsin.

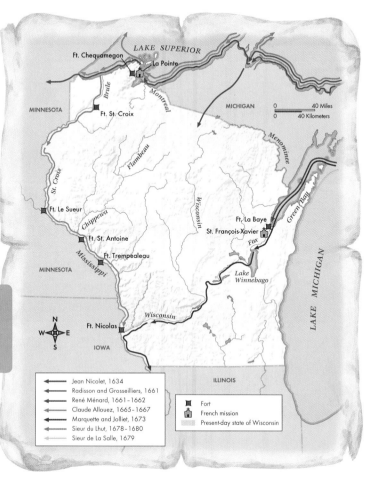

In 1832, a group of Native Americans battled U.S. forces in an attempt to hold on to land in southern Wisconsin. This conflict became known as the Black Hawk War.

Changing Times

White settlers poured into Wisconsin throughout the 1800s. Many came to mine lead, a metal used to make bullets and other items. This was a time of terrible hardship for the native people. Many died from diseases brought by the new settlers. The U.S. government also forced most Native Americans to give up their land. Many Native Americans were sent to live on **reservations** where the land was not good for growing food or hunting.

From Territory to State

Much of what is now the United States was once divided into large areas called **territories**. When the Wisconsin Territory was created in 1836, it included what are now Wisconsin, Minnesota, Iowa, and parts of North and South Dakota. Once an area had 60,000 residents, it could be considered for statehood. Wisconsin became the country's 30th state in 1848.

Timeline of Wisconsin Events

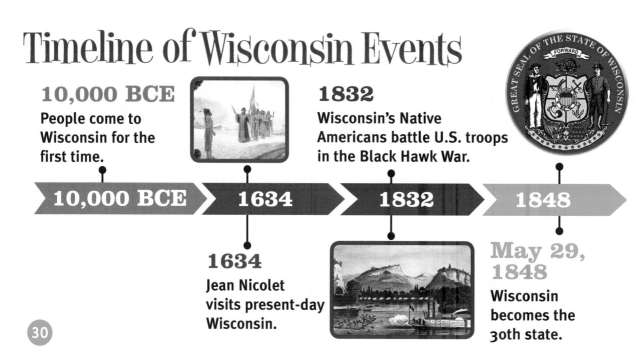

10,000 BCE
People come to Wisconsin for the first time.

1832
Wisconsin's Native Americans battle U.S. troops in the Black Hawk War.

10,000 BCE | 1634 | 1832 | 1848

1634
Jean Nicolet visits present-day Wisconsin.

May 29, 1848
Wisconsin becomes the 30th state.

Immigrants Arrive

Natural disasters and the hope of a better life brought tens of thousands of European **immigrants** to Wisconsin in the late 1800s. The largest group came from Germany. There were also many immigrants from Norway, Ireland, Poland, and Italy. Some came to farm. Others came to work in the lumber industry. Wisconsin had plenty of trees and the rivers and railroads to ship them on.

1967
African Americans in Milwaukee riot in response to unfair treatment and police brutality.

2003
Native American groups get permission to operate gambling establishments on reservations.

1919 **1967** **1976** **2003**

1919
The Green Bay Packers football team is established by E. L. "Curly" Lambeau and George Whitney Calhoun.

1976
Shirley Abrahamson becomes the first woman to be appointed to Wisconsin's Supreme Court.

In the years following the Civil War, many African Americans moved to Wisconsin from the South in search of better jobs.

The 20th Century

The 20th century was a period of tremendous change. During the Great Depression (1929–1939), many people lost their jobs and farms. To help them, the U.S. government created the Civilian Conservation Corps (CCC). CCC workers built parks, roads, and fences across Wisconsin. During World War II (1939–1945), Wisconsin factories built ships and submarines. When the war ended, factories switched to producing peacetime products.

Robert La Follette wasn't afraid to stand up to powerful people. His nickname was Fighting Bob.

The "Wisconsin Idea"

Robert M. La Follette (1855–1925) was a politician from Wisconsin. He saw that a small group of powerful people controlled many of the decisions made in the state. La Follette and his supporters believed citizens should be in charge. He promoted the "Wisconsin Idea." This put power into the hands of the voters. La Follette served as the governor of Wisconsin (1901–1906) and a U.S. senator (1906–1925).

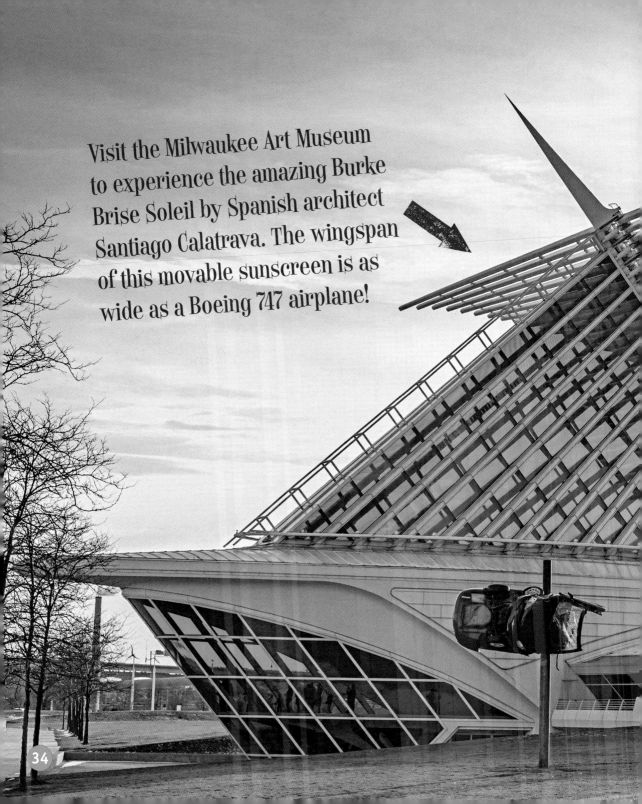

Visit the Milwaukee Art Museum to experience the amazing Burke Brise Soleil by Spanish architect Santiago Calatrava. The wingspan of this movable sunscreen is as wide as a Boeing 747 airplane!

CHAPTER 4

Culture

The list of things to see and do in Wisconsin is very long. Those who love the outdoors will find many great places to hike, swim, fish, camp, hunt, and canoe. Or how about seeing a concert or play at one of the state's many theaters? Many cities and towns are known for their farmers' markets. Wisconsin also has museums showcasing everything from art and history to logging, architecture, and geology. There's even a museum dedicated to mustard!

The Green Bay Packers

The people of Wisconsin are very proud of their pro football team, the Green Bay Packers, and there are many things that make the team unusual. Green Bay is the smallest city to have a National Football League (NFL) team. Also, the Packers are the only NFL team that is owned by its fans. The team has been around since 1919, making it one of the oldest in the NFL. The Packers have won more championships than any other team in the league.

Packers fans are proud to be known as Cheeseheads.

A team of stunt pilots zooms through the sky above Oshkosh.

Fun Things to Do

Wisconsin is home to a huge variety of exciting events. The Dane County Farmers' Market is held in Madison from April to November each year. It is one of the country's largest farmers' markets. Head north to Oshkosh for the Experimental Aircraft Association's annual fly-in. Wisconsin Dells calls itself the "waterpark capital of the world" and has lots of natural beauty too. Milwaukee hosts a different ethnic festival almost every summer weekend.

Widmer's Cheese Cellars in Theresa has been producing cheese using traditional methods since 1922.

The Dairy State—And So Much More!

The dairy industry is very important to Wisconsin. Although California has more cows, Wisconsin has more dairy farms and produces most of the country's cheese. Wisconsin is also known for other agricultural products, including cranberries, ginseng, and corn. Wisconsin factories make world-famous electronics, paper products, engines, power tools, and motorcycles.

Wonderful Water

Water is extremely important to Wisconsin's economy. Farmers depend on it to **irrigate** their crops. Vacationers enjoy lakes, rivers, and streams for boating, fishing, and water sports. Wisconsin's many **ports** make it easy to ship products and supplies. Over 30 million tons of goods come into Wisconsin each year through its port cities. Coal for power plants, iron ore for manufacturing, and salt for safe roads are just some of the products that travel through these ports.

A kayaker enjoys the sights of the Apostle Islands in Lake Superior.

Tasty Treats

Wisconsin is a food lover's paradise. When immigrants came to the state, they brought their favorite foods. Danish bakers brought the kringle, which is today the state pastry. Bratwurst, a type of sausage, came from Germany. Other popular Wisconsin foods include cheese curds, frozen custard, fried fish, and cream puffs as big as a person's head.

★ Wisconsin Cheese Dip

Make this tasty dip with fresh cheese from Wisconsin.

Ask an adult to help you!

Ingredients
2 tablespoons butter
2 tablespoons flour
1 teaspoon salt
1 cup milk
1 cup shredded cheddar cheese

Directions
With an adult's help, melt the butter in a saucepan over medium heat. Mix in the flour and salt. When it starts to bubble, slowly add the milk and continue stirring. Once the mixture starts to thicken, add the cheese. Continue stirring until the dip is smooth. Serve with veggies, chips, or other snacks.

An Incredible State

All year long, Wisconsin is a great place to live or visit. Ten thousand cross-country skiers take part in the American Birkebeiner race each February. In spring, Wisconsin hosts everything from a film festival to the Grilled Cheese Championship. Vacationers travel to Wisconsin in the summer months to enjoy water sports and the beautiful north woods. No matter what you like to do, you'll find it in Wisconsin! ★

Famous People

Laura Ingalls Wilder

(1867–1957) wrote the popular *Little House* books about her life in the woods of Wisconsin, the Kansas prairie, and the plains of South Dakota. She was born in Pepin.

Frank Lloyd Wright

(1867–1959) was one of America's most famous architects. He believed in "organic architecture," which meant that his buildings were designed to fit in well with their natural surroundings. He was from Richland Center.

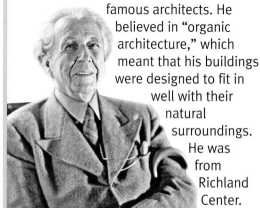

Aldo Leopold

(1887–1948) was a writer, scientist, and environmentalist. He is known by many as the father of wildlife conservation. He was a professor at the University of Wisconsin.

Georgia O'Keeffe

(1887–1986) was a painter who was known for capturing images of the Southwest, such as flowers and animal skulls. She was born in Sun Prairie.

Earl Lewis "Curly" Lambeau

(1898–1965) cofounded the Green Bay Packers. He played for the team and also coached it. The Packers' home stadium is named after him.

Ada Deer

(1935–) has worked hard to create social justice for Native Americans. She was the first woman to lead the U.S. Bureau of Indian Affairs. She was born in Keshena.

Henry "Hank" Aaron

(1934–) is considered one of the best baseball players ever. He played for the Milwaukee Braves for many years.

Eric Heiden

(1958–) is a speed skater who won five gold medals at the 1980 Winter Olympics. He is from Madison.

Paul Ryan

(1970–) is a politician who was a candidate for vice president in 2012. He was first elected to the U.S. House of Representatives in 1998 and became Speaker of the House in 2015. He is from Janesville.

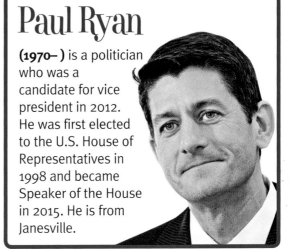

Did You Know That . . .

The first kindergarten classes in the United States were held in Wisconsin. German immigrants brought these classes to America.

Dairy is so important to Wisconsin that margarine, a type of butter substitute, was illegal in the state for many years.

There are 116 lakes in Wisconsin with the name Mud Lake.

Wisconsin's state capitol was built using 43 types of stone from all over the world.

Door County has more shoreline, state parks, and lighthouses than any other single county in the country.

Wisconsin produces more cranberries than any other state.

Did you find the truth?

F Europeans first came to Wisconsin in the 1800s.

T Wisconsin is home to one of the world's biggest annual music festivals.

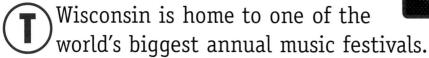

Resources

Books

Nonfiction

Blashfield, Jean F. *Wisconsin*. New York: Scholastic, 2014.

Loew, Patty. *Native People of Wisconsin*. Madison: Wisconsin Historical Society Press, 2015.

Parker, Bridget. *Wisconsin*. Mankato, MN: Capstone Press, 2017.

Fiction

North, Sterling. *Rascal*. New York: Dutton, 1963.

Wilder, Laura Ingalls. *Little House in the Big Woods*. New York: Harper & Row, 1932.

Visit this Scholastic website for more information on Wisconsin:

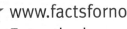 www.factsfornow.scholastic.com
Enter the keyword **Wisconsin**

Important Words

archaeologists (ahr-kee-AH-luh-jists) people who study the distant past

gorges (GOR-jiz) deep valleys or ravines

immigrants (IM-ih-gruhnts) people who move from one country to another and settle there

irrigate (IR-uh-gate) to supply water to crops by artificial means, such as channels and pipes

nomads (NOH-madz) people who move from place to place instead of settling down in permanent homes

peninsula (puh-NIN-suh-luh) an area of land that is almost entirely surrounded by water

ports (PORTS) harbors or bays where boats and ships can dock or anchor safely

reservations (rez-ur-VAY-shuhnz) areas of land set aside by government for a special purpose

territories (TER-ih-tor-eez) the lands and waters under the control of a nation

union (YOON-yuhn) an organized group of workers set up to help improve such things as working conditions, wages, and health benefits

Index

Page numbers in **bold** indicate illustrations.

About the Author

Vicky Franchino has lived in Wisconsin for most of her life. Although she is not a big fan of winter—and often dreams about moving someplace warm in January—she is a big fan of her home state! Vicky has been to a Packers game, but she has never worn a cheesehead. She doesn't live on a farm, but she has visited many of them. And, yes, Vicky has done her share of eating deep-fried foods served on a stick. She lives in Madison with her family. Raccoons and foxes sometimes walk through her yard, even though she lives in the city!